LET HIM
Love
YOU

TONYA MCDOWELL

Fowlkes Eagle Publishing, LLC

Let Him Love You

Copyright © 2019 by Tonya McDowell

All rights reserved. No part of this publication may be reproduced, stored or transmitted in any form or by any means, electronic, mechanical, photocopying, recording, scanning, or otherwise without written permission from the publisher. It is illegal to copy this book, post it to a website, or distribute it by any other means without permission.

Designations used by companies to distinguish their products are often claimed as trademarks. All brand names and product names used in this book and on its cover are trade names, service marks, trademarks and registered trademarks of their respective owners. The publishers and the book are not associated with any product or vendor mentioned in this book. None of the companies referenced within the book have endorsed the book.

The events and conversations in this book have been set down to the best of the author's ability, although some names have been withheld to protect the privacy of individuals.

Unless otherwise noted, all scripture quotations are from the New Living Translation of the Holy Bible.

Editing by Dr. Sharon Shaw

Book Cover Design by Deia Green

ISBN: 978-1-7332666-1-1 (Paperback)
ISBN: 978-1-7332666-0-4 (eBook)

Library of Congress Control Number: 2019909333

First Edition

Published by Fowlkes Eagle Publishing, LLC
P.O. Box 6412 Chesapeake, VA 23323
fowlkeseaglepublishing.com

To Love

*"Let us be glad and rejoice, and let us give honor to him.
For the time has come for the wedding feast of the Lamb,
and his bride has prepared herself."*
-Revelation 19:7

Contents

Preface — vii
Acknowledgement — ix
Love — 1
Faith — 13
Healing — 33
Giving — 45
Serving — 49
Afterword — 53
About the Author — 57

PREFACE

"God is love." (1 John 4:16) I knew this scripture was in the Bible. I just did not know which book and verse of the Bible. My aunt taught me that bible verse as a little girl, and it stuck with me all my life. It was not all the amazing stories about how Jesus healed the sick or raised the dead; it was that God is love. I do not know if it was because it made God "tangible" to me or if it was just a revelation. In any case, I knew what love was even if I did not fully understand who God was.

I knew love was real because I experienced it. I knew I had a family that loved and cherished me. My family adored me and I was the apple of my grandmother's eye. I was the only child for nine years, so I had a lot of attention and maybe was even a little spoiled. I knew that feeling of a full heart each time my mom held my hand when we got in the car. I knew every time my dad would sing, "You are so beautiful to me" that I was special and loved.

Most importantly, I knew how much I loved them. I could see love. I could feel love. I could give love. I could be loved. So to hear that God was love was all I ever needed to believe that God was whom He said He was. God is I AM. "I AM who I AM." (Exodus 3:14) I knew He was God and that God was real because LOVE is real.

What I love about love is that the feeling or experience of being loved is different for everyone. Love meets you where you are. Whether your love language is having someone buy you gifts or wash the dishes. Isn't that just like God to meet us where we are? Even if you had a troubled childhood or experienced a life-shattering divorce, most if not all have had an encounter with love, or should I say with God. Even if you are an unbeliever, you too have experienced God. So why do so many people still not believe? Is it due to their past hurts, current challenges, or lack of faith? I do not know the answer to that question. What I do know is that my life experiences were not meant just for me. They were meant to share God's love for us and to encourage someone to accept Jesus Christ as their Lord and Savior. After all, He did send His only begotten son to die on the cross for our sins and raised him on the 3rd day. "We love because he first loved us." (1 John 4:19)

ACKNOWLEDGMENT

I have to thank my husband for supporting me to be open and honest concerning our life together. It takes a strong man to deal with me. I am forever grateful that he waited to read the book until after it was published.

In addition, I would like to extend my appreciation to my spiritual leaders and the ministries that have enabled me to grow. I intentionally left out names to avoid any potential embarrassment, especially if I used scriptures out of context.

To my family and friends that have encouraged and supported me, thank you so much. I say this with a huge smile and a hug.

To all of "our" children *I love you.*

CHAPTER ONE
LOVE

"God is love." (1 John 4:16) He loves you just as you are. I am a witness to His love for us. If you all knew ALL of the SINS I have committed and the ones I am still trying to stop, most of you would not even touch this book. I have DONE some things in my lifetime. "God's law was given so that all people could see how sinful they were. But as people sinned more and more, God's wonderful grace became more abundant." (Romans 5:20) I am so thankful to God for His abundant grace and love for us all. My goal is to be as transparent as possible, so with that, please do not judge me. If you do judge, please do it in love. I am sensitive. Seriously, my passion and my purpose are to share God's love despite our faults and failures, He still loves us even with all the skeletons in our closets.

Let me start by saying, I did not grow up in church. I always knew that Jesus died on the cross for my sins. My aunts and uncle would take me to church with them. My mom did not routinely take me to church. I knew church was a place I enjoyed going to, and sometimes I would even go with my friends or even by myself.

I never knew all the little church rules, such as holding your finger up when you needed to go to the restroom or why the ushers wore white gloves. I still do not know the answers to my questions, and I really do not care to know. I need to know about my relationship with Christ; not tradition or religion.

I remember accepting Jesus as my Lord and Savior and at the age of 13 during a weekly community church outreach event for teens. We watched a "holiness or hell" video with images of people being caught up in the rapture and others left behind awoken my spiritual senses. Tears started running down my cheeks as if I had been cutting onions. I immediately accepted Jesus Christ as my Lord and Savior. I will never forget that heavy cry. Looking back now, I question if I accepted Jesus out of fear, or for His love for me? To be honest, I think it was fear, but what a difference it would have been if it was out of love.

After I got saved, I read the Bible, prayed, and made the decision to stay pure. Shoot! I was not trying to go to Hell for anybody. I graduated from high school and fell in love. Yes, you know what happened next. My flesh got weak, and curiosity killed the cat. Guess who I called immediately to tell of my fornication escapade? It should have been Jesus, but it was my mom. I called her at 2:00 AM and told her I lost my virginity. To help put things in perspective, my mom had me when she was young and single. She has always been my best friend and a confidant. I told her what I had done. I remember her words like it was yesterday. She said, "Are you ok? Did you use protection?" Her next comment was the kicker. "I thought you were going to wait." All I could say was "yes" and "yes" and "I did too."

In my heart of hearts, I wanted to wait until I got married. I wanted to live a holy life. My goal was to get married at 22, have my first baby at 25, and live happily ever after with my soul mate. I felt so guilty, even when the person promised to love me forever. I felt like the biggest sinner on the planet. Still, I wanted to do it (SEX) again, and I did again and again and again. The flesh is weak.

"I don't really understand myself, for I want to do what is right, but I don't do it. Instead, I do what I hate. But if I know that what I am doing is wrong, this shows that the law is good. So I am not the one doing wrong; it is the sin living in me that does it." (Romans 7:15-17) I felt just like that Bible verse, and I had so many emotions, so I dropped out of college, joined the military, and received orders to San Antonio, Texas. I was confused, guilty, and lost. I let my emotions make decisions for me. My family thought I had lost my mind. My grandma said, "That military is going to own you just as if you were one of their pens." The biggest lesson I learned during that phase of my life was not to let your emotions or how you feel in a moment make decisions for you. It can cost you your life.

Soon after I moved to Texas, my relationship ended. I was living in a military dorm and meeting new friends. I enjoyed being on my own. I wanted to find a church to attend and grow as a Christian, so I visited a local Baptist church. The ushers welcomed me with open arms, the choir could sing, and the message was uplifting. Towards the end of the service, it was time for Holy Communion, and the ushers were passing the bread and grape juice. When the plate got to me, the usher looked at me and said, "Are you baptized?" I said, "No," and the usher looked at me like I was the scum of the Earth and said, "You can't touch the plate or take communion."

I was so embarrassed and hurt. I had never heard of such a thing, but remember I did not grow up in church. I had taken communion dozens of times and never had any issues. I felt unworthy. It took a while for me to visit another church because that sense of unworthiness lasted for years. To this day, I have to continually remind myself that I am the righteousness of God in Christ. "God made him who had no sin to be sin for us, so that in him we might become the righteousness of God." (2 Corinthians 5:21)

Now, I wish I could say that I found a new church and walked into my purpose. That is not how life works. Every situation, every wrong decision, every right choice, every joyful occasion, and every heartbreak prepares us for our future and develops us to be whom God has called us to be. "And we know that all things work together for good to them that love God, to them who are called according to his purpose." (Romans 8:28 KJV) Many times when this scripture is quoted, we say for MY good, but a woman of faith shared with me that it is for the greater good, not just for me. I am sharing my experiences to help others be free from whatever is keeping them from God's love. This book is for the greater good. By no means, am I a Bible scholar. I only knew one verse for the majority of my life. "God is love." (1 John 4:16) I am so grateful to have known that one verse.

For this reason, one of my best friends, and trust me I have a lot of them, asked me to find a Bible verse and read it during a women's day service at her church. I was honored and scared to death at the same time. You would have thought she had asked me to preach at a revival. I only knew one line from the Bible "God is love." and on the way to the service, I could not remember the verse. I did not want to embarrass my friend or fail at the opportunity to read scripture in church on a Sunday morning. I went to church occasionally and did not know church etiquette. I was sweating and praying the entire way to church. I get there, and she tells me that I am sitting in the pulpit right beside the minister who was preaching that day. I had never stood on a pulpit before, and now she wanted this sinner to sit in the pulpit! Now, nine times out of ten, I had probably cussed my husband out just before I got in the car on the way to the church. She wanted me of all people to sit beside a Woman of God. I was thinking, "Oh, no. God is going to strike me dead right here on the pulpit."

Before I trembled my way to the pulpit, my dear friend handed me the service program. Guess what the scripture was on the front of the program? "God is love." (1 John 4:16) Out of all the verses in the Bible, the only verse I knew happened to be on the program. It gave me so much peace and joy. The program cover confirmed that I selected the right scripture, but it also showed me how much God loved me. He loved me so much so that even if I got to the microphone and forgot the Bible verse, all I needed to do was look at the program. God was thinking of me the entire time. Even before, I was asked to read the Bible verse and after I started searching frantically to find the verse, and also during my argument with my husband; God had already had my back. Isn't that love? Our heavenly Father, the Creator of the heavens and the Earth, thinks of us all with intent. We are His children. He loves us. He loves you. He loves me. "Give thanks to the God of heaven. His faithful love endures forever." (Psalms 136:36)

When it was time for me to read the verse, I had new found confidence. I shared how unqualified I felt and how the Lord strengthened and encouraged me. I did not miss the mark. I was reading the perfect verse. When you look at your life and think about all the times, God was with you. Please take a moment and think about that car accident that you miraculously avoided or the time when you were at the right place at the right time. It was not a coincidence or by chance. It was the goodness of the Lord, guiding and protecting you. "Give thanks to our Lord, for He is good." (Psalm 118:29) Despite me being me. He still wanted to use me for His glory. I thought that verse was to be used to encourage someone else on a Sunday morning, but God had so much more in store. "His thoughts are not our thoughts, and his ways are not our ways." (Isaiah 55:8) He wanted that to be an experience that would remind me of His love for me, be the catalyst to my first book, and most importantly be able to share to the masses His love for them.

First, I think it is essential for you to have a little insight into who I am. For those who KNOW me may nod and smile. For those who do not, I think it will provide more substance to my experiences. For those who THINK they know me, they may never look at me the same after reading this book. With that said, I am stepping out on faith and praying that sharing my experience blesses more than it hurts. I want to enlighten and not disappoint. After this book is published, I am sure there will be critics but, when you are fulfilling your destiny, you learn how to dismiss the distractions. That drop of knowledge was a bonus.

Seriously, I love people. My family and friends are my heart. I am loyal and compassionate. I am a giver. My friends say I am funny or crazy. I am extremely literal. I am a cross between Rose and Blanche from Golden Girls. Seventy-five percent Rose and twenty-five percent Blanche to be exact. I do not want anyone to get the wrong impression of me, so I have to be precise.

Also, I am not too fond of feet; except baby feet. Well, baby feet under the age of one. Once they start walking, they are immediately in the anti-feet zone. My hobbies are shopping and event planning. Okay, I love shoes too. I feel guilty writing that, but I do like wearing a gorgeous pair of stilettos. I am a private person. I do not have social media accounts (that may change once this book is published), or pictures of my family in my cubicle or future corner office on the top floor. If you are not in my circle, you are NOT in my circle.

You will not know what I am wearing to date night or what I am ordering from take-out in real time.

I think that is one of the reasons it took me so long to start writing this book. I did not want anyone in my business. In actuality, I never wanted to expose my dysfunction. My side of the room is messy, and my cubicle is immaculate. I can live with dirty dishes in the sink, but my pet peeve is a filthy microwave. We want people to see what we want them to see. Even behind my smiling face and perfectly sculptured eyebrows, I still have a story. We all have a story. My sister and cousin always told me that my family should have a reality show because it would be a hit. I said, "No way." I would be too embarrassed if the world saw my drama.

Despite my dysfunction, I am an optimistic extrovert. I am not the person to call if you want to have a pity party. I am going to turn any negative into a positive and tell you that God's got your back no matter what you are going through. I guess that is why I do not like bad news. Everyone knows not to tell me bad news because I take on the sadness. I will be up all night thinking about the victims and hurting for the victims. I do not watch the news because I already know that people are dying. They are dying physically, emotionally, psychologically, spiritually, economically, and politically.

Society has become so numb to the bad news that it makes saying a 16-year old died last night just like saying the weather is 70 degrees. How did we get to the point where people dying senselessly is ok? It is effortless to talk about problems and what we do not like, but it is a challenge to talk about the solutions. How can we fix it? I try to focus on what

I can do to help make the world a better place. It may be volunteering, encouraging someone, writing a book, starting a non-profit, or simply sharing a testimony.

God uses people to bless people. He has perfect plans for our lives. My favorite Bible verse is Jeremiah 29:11. "For I know the plans I have for you," declares the Lord, plans to prosper you and not to harm you, plans to give you hope and a future." (Jeremiah 29:11 NIV) This verse gives me so much assurance that God is not out to punish us for doing wrong or for not going to church every Sunday, or not reading the Bible. He wants to bless us and prosper us, not do us in. Time for a praise break. Thank you, Jesus! I am so glad we serve a good God.

"No power in the sky above or in the earth below-indeed, nothing in all creation will ever be able to separate us from the love of God that is revealed in Christ Jesus our Lord." (Romans 8:39) We should rejoice that God is not like man. His love is unfailing. When you get a hold of His love for you, your life will never be the same. I am a living witness that His love is real and permanent. His love is pure, and He does not love out of obligation.

I am forever grateful for His love for us. His love for us was revealed to me, even more, one day during a shopping trip. I have to admit; I have a keen sense of smell. I can smell things good or bad from a mile away. I have sons and boys can be stinky. This heightened sense has caused me to create a habit of holding my breath every time I am near a foul odor. I know that sounds crazy and weird, but in my mind, if I smell something stinky, I taste something stinky. I think that is disgusting. Your nose and throat are connected, so this makes perfect sense to me. Holding my breath has come in handy when someone leaves the window locks on, and I need fresh air right away if you know what I mean. As I approached the elevator to enter the second level entry of the mall, a homeless man enters the elevator with me, and I instantly go into breath holding mode. It is clear he is going through a rough time. His clothes were hanging on by a thread, and his hands showed the effects of constant exposure to the elements.

As shallow as this may be, my first thoughts were "How can I hold my breath the entire ride up to the second floor without passing out?" I know this sounds heartless, but it was at that moment when I heard from the Lord in a still voice that said, "I love him just as much as I love you." It hit me like a ton of bricks. I felt horrible and enlightened at the same time. How dare I have my nose in the air (literally) at one of God's children? I had already known how much God loved me in spite of me, but when He said that he loved that man just as much as he loved me, it put things in an entirely new perspective.

Just think about God's love for you. It is agape love; which is the highest form of love. This experience also gave me another revelation of love we should have for one another. "This is my commandment: Love each other in the same way I have loved you." (John 15:12 NLT) Imagine if we all loved as our Heavenly Father commands us to love. The world would be such a better place. People would ask, "How are you doing?" with compassion, not just the generic "How are you?" as they zoom, pass you. People would give without expecting anything in return. People would borrow money and pay it back. I thank God for my elevator moment. The next time someone cuts you off, lies about you, or beg for money at the traffic light, remember God loves them just as much as He loves you.

Last but not least, love yourself. I thank God for my sister, reminding me of the importance of loving you. One of the things that I admire most about my sister is that she does not need validation from anyone. I think that is a direct reflection of the amount of love she has for herself. Hypothetically speaking, I am shopping with my mom. I see a shirt that I really like and say, "Do you like this"? My mom response is, "It looks a little old fashion." I hang the shirt back on the rack with disappointment in my eyes. My sister, on the other hand, would not have even asked my mom's opinion and would have walked to the cash register with a smile on her face.

It is liberating to know that what other people think about you is just their thoughts and does not validate, or represent who you are as an individual. I am reminded of a Bible verse: "And the very hairs on your head are all numbered. So don't be afraid; you are more valuable to God than a whole flock of sparrows." (Matthew 10:30-31) Know that you are of valued not only in God's eyes but in your own. Love yourself because it is hard to receive God's love or love others if you do not love you. Love is vital, and God is Love!

CHAPTER TWO
FAITH

"So then faith cometh by hearing, and hearing by the word of God." (Romans 10:17) Let me tell you there are times in my life when the only thing that helps me to get through a tough time is a word from God. It is so encouraging to know that during those rough times, my faith increased the more I listen to God's word.

Truthfully, we should listen, read, and meditate on God's word daily. Faith is knowing that things will get better, regardless of your circumstances. God has your best interest at heart and has given each of us a portion of faith. We have to believe and hope for the best at all times. Life is going to put you in situations that will make you uncomfortable, so we need to develop our faith, so we are equipped to handle them all.

I have to admit that the thing that brings me closer to God's word every day is my MARRIAGE. I love my husband. There are times when he gets on my nerves. Ok, I get on his nerves too, but he really gets on mine, LOL. My marriage has been the means to my faith development and increased prayer life. God has used my marriage and my connection with my husband to teach me even more about what love is and who God is. "Love is patient and kind. Love is not jealous or boastful or proud." (1 Corinthians 13:4) God is all of those things, and so much more.

As I mentioned, my marriage is a testimony. I am going to share some of my marital hurdles, but I cannot tell EVERYTHING for two reasons. Reason #1, I want to stay married. Reason #2, only a fool tells all his feelings. (Proverbs 29:11) My husband and I have had many challenges. I have wanted to divorce him more times than I can think. If he blinked twice, I was telling him I was leaving him and telling everybody else too. Thank God for keeping us together despite our foolishness.

Our Love Story

I met Jeff in 2002 on a Wednesday night, one week after my 20th birthday. Jeff and a group of his friends were leaving the club when one of his friends suggested they stop by my best friend's house. I was there with my BFF and her friends' playing cards. The guys came over, and when Jeff walked in, he stood out. He was tall and handsome with a charming smile. Immediately, I said, "Hey, come talk to me." I usually would never approach a guy. There was just something about him. We talked for about 2 hours and had a great conversation. He asked me for my phone number, and I gave it to him. He called me when he got home at about 4:00 am and said that he was calling to verify that I gave him the right number. Ugh! I was immediately turned off. Why would I talk to you for 2 hour just to give you the wrong number?

In my mind, he was lame, and maybe he was used to girls giving him the wrong number, so I lost all interest. Nobody wants to date somebody nobody wants. He continued to call me for two weeks, and I never answered the phone. He eventually left a voicemail that stole my heart. He said, "Hey, I see you never answer the phone when I call, so I am going to stop calling you." As I was listening, I thought, yes! He gets that I am not interested. Then he said, "No, I am just joking I am going to call you right back." LOL. I busted out laughing, and to this day, the thought of that message still puts a smile on my face. His persistence and sense of humor got my attention. I called him back.

We had our first date at Feather N Fin Chicken & Seafood. It is a local fast food restaurant that most people would not go to for a first date, but I was still in the Air Force stationed in Texas, craving some hometown food. Jeff and I were looking sharp. He had on a matching jean outfit. I had on a caramel colored dress that complimented my complexion. He did not know where we were going, but I had plans to go out with my friends after the date.

Looking back, that was a little mean of me because he was expecting to spend more time with me and we were at a fast food spot. After our first date, my car broke down. Jeff offered to rent me a car for a week. He gave me three hundred dollars. We had never kissed or had any sexual contact (just wanted to be clear so people would not get the wrong impression). Jeff's generosity towards me after knowing me for less than a month showed me that he was serious about getting to know me, he was caring, and he was capable of being a provider. To this day, I tell Jeff that three hundred dollars was the best investment he ever made, LOL. We continued to talk and date, but I was 20, and my heart was towards someone else. I told Jeff that we should be friends, and he agreed. When it was time for me to drive back to Texas, he offered to ride with me and take the 3-day bus back to Virginia. I was extremely grateful to Jeff for his sacrifice. When he went back to Virginia, I missed him and asked if we should take our relationship to the next level. He said that I lived 1,600 miles away and that we should be friends. I understood.

A few months later, a close male friend from Virginia moved to Texas. It was great to see a familiar face in Texas. Most of my Air Force friends had received orders to other locations, so it was comforting to have a friend in the area. Our friendship grew into a relationship. I was head over heels infatuated. I mean, I could not even think straight.

Shortly after, I was pregnant. Earlier in the book, I mentioned that my parents were not married, and it was not meant to be demeaning or judgmental. I ended up pregnant around the same age my mom was when she had me. I did the same thing my parents and grandparents did. It is important to recognize negative generational cycles early and break the chain.

During my second trimester, my boyfriend broke up with me and moved back to Virginia. I was heartbroken. Jeff called to check on me, and I told him what had happened. He said, "I love you and your unborn child. I want to be with you." I was in awe. I could not believe he still wanted me regardless of me being pregnant with another man's child. It was like a scene from a movie. It was God once again showing me, unconditional love.

It was a type of love and support I never experienced before. I have to be honest; if Jeff had told me that he had a little one on the way, I would have said, "Congratulations and best wishes on your new relationship."

Not Jeff, he truly loved me.

Our Fight

March 4th, 2005, Jeff and I got married when my baby was one and a half years old. A year after we were married, we had baby number two. I was 24 years old, married with two kids, working, and going to school full time. The honeymoon was over. Things were getting real, real fast. Notice I said my baby at the beginning of this paragraph. It was on purpose and one of our biggest hurdles. Despite Jeff buying my maternity clothes when I was pregnant with "my" baby, visiting me in the hospital when I went in pre-term labor, making bottles, and providing for us, something had changed.

Once "our" baby was born, I begin to notice that Jeff had

an extra sparkle in his eye for "our" baby, and he treated "my" baby differently. The kids were 2 and a half years apart. At those ages, you cannot tickle one and not the other. You cannot take "my" baby's toys away as a punishment and not the other.

The more I noticed the differences, the more I called Jeff out on it, which created an instant division for our family. They were both my children. I loved them both dearly. I felt as if I had to compensate for the lack of compassion Jeff had for "my" baby. Every time Jeff said something to our kids, especially "my" baby, I went in instant defense mode.

After a while, our kids started to notice the dysfunction because I continued to highlight the issues and never supported Jeff's role as a father to our sons. I was concerned that the boys would be jealous of one another due to the blended family issues we were experiencing, so I tried to reward them for acts of kindness toward each other. I called it "Brotherly Love." Each time they were genuinely kind, I would give them 25 cents. At the end of the week, they received the money they earned and hopefully solidified their bond.

Brotherly Love was working well, but marital love was going down fast. My heart was growing bitter towards my husband. The only thing I knew to do was fuss and cuss him out. If you say or do something to hurt me, I am going to say or do something ten times more hurtful to you (pray for me). With that said, our arguments were not small debates; they were wars. We constantly argued no matter where we were and no matter who was around. If you were with us for more than 10 minutes, you would have been in for a show.

We argued during date night at Red Lobster about who got the biggest crab leg. We argued about the Valentine's Day candy he ate prior to giving me the candy and tried to make it look as if he did not eat any. We argued about him being in the barbershop when he said he was down the street from the house. We argued about him not coming to "my" son's birthday party because he felt as though I spent too much money on the party (that hurt). We argued about the house he did not want to buy, and I said we were buying it regardless (that was rough, do not judge me). We argued about him not picking me up from the front door of the church when it was raining. We argued about not going to church. We argued about going to church late. We argued about me not cooking.

Oh Yes! My desire not to cook has caused a number of battles and one that continues to be a sensitive topic. There is one cooking battle in particular that truly stands out; it was right after "our" baby boy was born. It was a hot Saturday morning in the middle of the summer. I had recently bought Jeff a twelve hundred dollar 1990 Box Chevy Caprice. It was purple, so I named it the Purple Monster.

He purchased three thousand dollars' worth of 22-inch rims with Pirelli tires. I thought that was a total waste of money because we were saving to buy a house.

He woke up and said, "Where is breakfast?" I said, "There is some cereal downstairs." He said, "You are a horrible mother and wife. What kind of mother does not feed her children?" I said, "OK." I went to the kitchen and got a dozen eggs. I then went outside and began to "serve" breakfast. I said, "Here are your scrambled eggs" smack right down on the hood of his car. "Here are your fried eggs" Smack "Here are your boiled eggs" Smack "Here are your sunny side up eggs" etc. until I egged his entire car and rims. To this day, I do not know how long it took for him to clean all those eggs off his car. He got me back by pouring cold water on me in our brand new king size bed that was a wedding gift from my mother. I am not sure if you have ever seen the stain that water can leave on your brand new white mattress, but it is disgusting.

Our childish behavior and downright disrespect for one another left more than just a stain on our mattress; the residue spread to our kids and marriage like wildfire. Jeff began to spend 5 out of 7 days out with his friends, and I was going out to the club whenever I felt like it. We had more "me" time than "we" time. The more I cried out for Jeff's attention; the more he pulled away.

I decided to put the kids in counseling because they were demonstrating severe anxiety. I did not want my kids to be hurt men carrying all that baggage as adults. I wanted them to be God-fearing husbands and fathers that knew how to handle conflict in a healthy way. As the children healed, my heart grew cold and hard towards Jeff, and I am sure he felt the same way. After ten years of marriage, I decided it was time for a divorce. Ten represents a test in the Bible, and I was failing.

* * *

Our Therapy

Sex therapy was our therapy for a while, but that was short lived. No pun intended, LOL. Make-up sex placed a temporary bandage on the real issues. We never addressed anything. We would "make up," and two days later, we would be right back arguing. It was time for me to get off the emotional roller coaster. In January 2015, the boys and I moved in with my mom. Jeff stayed in the house. I thought he would call me a hundred times a day and beg for his family back. I made the wrong assumption because it took over a week for him to call. He finally called and invited the boys and me over for a visit.

In my imagination, I thought he would have new toys for the kids, a dozen roses for me, and my favorite food (pizza). It felt great driving up to my home. At that moment, there was an inkling of hope that my marriage could be saved. As I walked into the house, I saw something I never expected. Jeff was in the house playing cards with friends and drinking a beer and having the time of his life. He was not sad or depressed. He looked as if he did not even miss his family. He gave the kids and me a quick wave then I snapped. I cussed him out in front of his friends and the kids. I took the boys and blocked his cell number and went back to my mom's house. I was hurt and disappointed.

A few days went by, and during this time, I prayed and cried and listened to gospel music. Jeff called me and asked if

I could meet him for lunch. At lunch, we talked about our issues. I gave him an ultimatum it was either we seek professional counseling or divorce attorneys. He said, "You cannot put a man's back against the wall. We are going to dig underneath or climb over the wall" in his stern manly voice. I could not think of a cool comeback wall analogy, so I just said, "Well, the ball is in your court. Here is the number to the counselor. If you are serious about this marriage; call, schedule, and pay for each session."

At that time, I wanted him to show some initiative, but I also wanted to protect my heart and my finances at the same time, so I told him that we should put the house on the market. The house was always a point of contention, and in the back of my mind, it would be one less thing to fight over during a divorce. Jeff scheduled the counseling session. The boys and I moved back in, so we could start preparing the house to be listed.

Before our first session, the counselor asked us to do an online assessment to see our strengths and weakness as a couple. Guess what our issues were? Communications and parenting. Jeff and I both agreed that the online assessment was 100% accurate. Our counselor was a Christian, but she was not the churchy type. She was real, wise, and fair. She had been married for over 30 years and understood the challenges of a blended family. She listened to both of us and told me that I had unrealistic expectations of marriage. I thought after ten years of being with someone; you get to a point where there is smooth sailing, which is not the case. That is not even the case in life because even when the seas are calm, there are still swells and ripples.

She told me that I had one foot out and one foot in the marriage. I needed to commit to rebuilding. Jeff needed to speak up. Years of me making every major decision and Jeff just rolling with it caused him to resent me. There were times I should have listened to him, and I did not because I grew up in a household where my mom made the decisions. To be a little more transparent; my main issue was the lack of respect I had for my husband. Later, I learned that I did not want to be Vashti from the Bible and lose my crown (Read the Book of Esther). Jeff had traditional expectations on how our family should operate. We did not realize how much our childhood played a part in our marriage and how we raised our children. My dad always told me to do what he says and not what he does, but the reality is that children do what we do. As parents, we need to do better because our kids are watching.

Our counselor also helped us focus on our positive characteristics. Look, I have to admit this helped me put things in perspective. My husband is "The Man." He works 10 to 12 hours a day 5-6 days per week, does all the laundry for the entire family, makes the groceries, pays the bills, cleans, helps the kids with homework, takes them to practice, and most importantly, loves his family. I do everything else. LOL

Thankfully, counseling saved our marriage. We went once a week for six months and looked forward to each session. Jeff was even talking about our counseling sessions in the barber shop. Our light bulb moment was when our counselor gave us the results from our love language assessment (The 5 Love Languages, by Gary Chapman). We both assumed that we knew each other's love language. We had been together 13 years in total.

Truth be told, we did not even know our own love language. I just knew my love language was quality time because I complained about him spending too much time with his friends. We thought his love language was acts of service because I am not the most domesticated wife. The assessment revealed that my love language was physical touch. Jeff's love language was words of affirmation, so the entire time we had not loved each other the way we receive love. I had been using my words to break him down instead of building him up, and it was not enough for him to be home watching a movie with me. I needed his touch. At that moment, I broke down and cried like a baby. I apologized for not loving him the way he needed to be loved.

That was a pivotal point in our marriage and for us as individuals. It made me think back to when my mom would hold my hand in the car, and the sound of laughter each time my dad tickled me under my arms. It also gave me a deeper understanding of why make-up sex worked as long as it did. I now know why I am a full-fledged "Hugger." I greet people with hugs. I hug people when I am excited. I hug when I am sad. It all made so much more sense. Knowing our love language made us fall back in love with intensity and a deeper level of intimacy. We were committed to the marriage and each other like never before.

* * *

Our Legacy

Jeff and I were newlyweds all over again. Even with all the love in the air, the house would not sell. This time the house was not listed to protect my financial portfolio. We wanted to sell the house to start our new chapter, leave the past in the past, and to upgrade. The house was a charming starter home. It was a three bedroom, two bathroom ranch style home in a great neighborhood and school district. We lowered the price of the house and stood in the foyer, praying for the house to sell. The kids were even praying for the house to sell. The house still did not sell.

I ran into a wise friend while shopping. She said, "You know why your house has not sold? It is because you have not started looking for a new one." I said, "Girl, I am not going to be stuck with two mortgages." She said, "You are going to know it is your house when you walk in the door. The sun will shine through the house."

I jokingly told our real estate agent what she said, and he said, "Just look online, so when we sell your house, I will know what type of home you are looking for." I looked online that very day, and a house came on the market that caught my attention. Jeff always wanted an all brick two-story home. This house was all brick and two stories. It was in the same school district as our house current home. I called Jeff and the agent and said, "We need to see the house today."

We went to the house which was less than 5 minutes

from our current home. Just as my friend said, I walked in the foyer and knew that this was our home. The sun pierced through each window like a divine glow from heaven. Not only was the house bright from all of the natural light, but, it was 100 degrees in the house. The house was a foreclosure, so it did not have any power and in need of minor repairs. The house was our dream home, with six bedrooms and three bathrooms. The purchase of this home would be a serious upgrade from sixteen hundred square feet to four thousand square feet.

The house had features I always wanted, but never verbalized like an extra set of steps in the kitchen and the perfect sized kitchen island. I only saw those home features on TV. I never imagined that I could have it for myself. I said, "Let's put in an offer today for the full asking price." Jeff was hesitant because the house needed work. Plus, we had not sold the first house. We even met the neighbor as if we already owned the home. He recommended that we offer twenty percent below asking because it was a foreclosure. I did not agree; this house was a gem. It was built just for us. I showed Jeff the prices of homes with those features, none of which were in our price range and were in the wrong school districts. Plus, most new homes were built with vinyl siding and half the square footage. Finally, Jeff and I were on the same page. We agreed to buy the house.

We were our real estate agent's first customers. God gave him wisdom for his first purchase. He explained that the listing stated that the bank would not accept closing cost assistance and that we should request a 30-day closing to make our offer more appealing. The next few days were exciting and nerve-racking at the same time. During that time, my big cousin told me not to worry, and if the house was meant for us, it was for us. We visited the house a few times. Each time the kitchen countertops were filled with real estate agents' business cards. The house was so popular that when Jeff went to look at a new development, the agent there was talking about our dream home. We received a call from our agent who told us there were multiple offers and we were in a bidding war. We had to give our best and final offer that afternoon.

Jeff and I prayed. We agreed on a price and put it in God's hands. A few days went by; I drove to work listening to a song with a chorus line, "something big is about to happen." It touched my soul. I knew that good news was on the way in my spirit. That day my agent notified me that we won the bidding war. Someone offered four thousand dollars more than what we offered, but they asked for closing costs assistance, which was non-negotiable.

Next, we needed to secure financing within 30 days. The credit union we chose had a reputation for not closing on time, but they had the lowest interest rates. The plan was to have Jeff use his VA loan since I used mine for our first home. Two weeks into the process, we learned that Jeff was a few months shy of the 2-year active duty requirement to obtain a VA loan. We were disappointed, but God made a way out of no way. We found out that I could have two VA loans. We would have to make a substantial down payment to keep both homes within the VA home loan threshold.

Guess who had all the money needed to buy his wife our dream home? My husband. The same husband that I put down and said I did not need. The same husband I told that if he left us, nothing would change, not even my zip code because I could afford to pay for everything by myself. He had all the money we needed to pay the closing cost. I am not talking a few thousand dollars, but tens of thousands. We closed on our house in July 2015 and "our" sons handed us our keys. God is awesome!

The excitement of closing on the new house did not stop there. Since the first house did not sell before the purchase of the new house; we decided to rent our first home. The same month we were moving into our new home, our friends asked if they could rent our home. I was skeptical because friends and money do not mix. The couple was loving, mature, and responsible. They needed a ranch style home for mobility and comfort, so our first home was perfect. We moved out, and they moved in the same day. Jeff and I never had to pay two mortgages, and we were establishing generational wealth for our family. "Good people leave an inheritance to their grandchildren, but the sinner's wealth passes to the godly." (Proverbs 13:22)

We wanted to be a blessing to our friends as well. We charged them less rent than the average cost of a home in our neighborhood. Our blessings are not just meant for us. It is important to mention that Jeff and I had humble beginnings as children and as a young couple. Our first apartment had two bedrooms and a one-person kitchen. When we started looking for homes, they were all in low-income neighborhoods because that was all we could afford. We even put a thousand dollar earnest deposit down to have a house built, but my mom and aunt were concerned for our safety. My mom pleaded with us to cancel the contract and offered us five hundred dollars to withdraw the contract; which we accepted.

Once again, God was using someone to bless, protect, and usher us toward building a legacy for our family years before we even knew what He had in store. When I walk up the stairs, I say, "Thank You, Jesus." I do not say it every time because I lose my breath going up and down those stairs, but I have to give God the praise because when I look back on where we started, I am amazed.

Faith Continued

"He replied, "Because you have so little faith. Truly I tell you, if you have faith as small as a mustard seed, you can say to this mountain, 'Move from here to there,' and it will move. Nothing will be impossible for you." (Matthew 17:20). For years, I did not know why we needed to pray to move mountains because I am so literal, so to clarify for those individuals like myself. The mountain is a metaphor for your cause or challenge. We are all given a portion of faith. It takes faith to believe in God. It takes faith to believe in love. It takes faith to go to counseling with a broken heart. It takes faith to fail and try again. Life takes faith. Granted, I was happy that

God healed my marriage and blessed us with a home and rental property, but, that was not the big "it" for me. What took the cake for me was how much my faith had grown. My mustard seed had a bud!

In six months, I went from wanting to divorce my husband with plans to move to an apartment to owning two homes and falling back in love with my husband. God showed me how much love He had for me even when I had a personal agenda, a master plan, and praying for a house to sell designated for my great-grandchildren. Just like His word says He does more than what we ask. "Now unto Him, that is able to do exceeding abundantly above all that we ask or think, according to the power that worketh in us." (Ephesians 3:20) We have to stop putting God in a box when He can do the impossible. Stop thinking small. I am a living testimony that if you get a hold of this faith thing and God's love for you; you will move mountains. Those around you will see God in you.

I can be walking down the hall at work or shopping in the mall and people will tell me that I have a good spirit or bubbly personality and I say "Thank you. It is nothing but God." As my faith grew, my confidence grew. Let me tell you; I can be at a wedding or a child's birthday and say "hey guess what?" I wanted to divorce my husband, but God had a better plan. Nine times out of ten, they are encouraged by my testimony. Some have even asked for our counselor's phone number.

One Sunday in church, my Bishop made a statement that God has blessed you tremendously, and He has more. I was thinking about what more can it be. Jeff and I were in a good place. Our kids were healthy. Our careers were on the right track. There were a few dollars in the bank. Our families were good. My heart just smiled, knowing that I was ready for whatever was to come because faith prepares you.

CHAPTER THREE
HEALING

"But he was wounded for our transgressions, he was bruised for our iniquities: the chastisement of our peace was upon him, and with his stripes, we are healed." (Isaiah 53:5 KJV) When I was young, I rarely heard about people diagnosed with cancer and never had a classmate with food allergies. Nowadays, a cancer diagnosis is just as common as getting the flu. Do not take peanut butter cookies to the school because of the sheer amount of children with peanut allergies. As an adult, all of my maternal aunts were diagnosed with cancer, my grandfather died from cancer, and the majority of his 13 siblings died from cancer. I have lost friends to cancer and other illnesses. Despite what we see, the doctor reports, and current medical journal suggestions, we should trust what God's word says about healing. We are healed.

In the summer of 2016, my mom decided to take the

BRCA gene testing because of the prevalence of cancer in our family. Her test came back positive for the BRCA 2 gene mutation. BRCA 2 gene mutation can cause an increased risk of breast, ovarian, and prostate cancer. It is suggested to have prophy- lactic surgery to decrease the risk of cancer. (Public Health Announcement: If you have a family history of cancer, please get tested for the BRCA gene. It can save your life and the lives of those you love. If you have any cancer symptoms and the doctors do not think it is cancer. Please request additional testing. Early detection is key.) My mom told me I should take the test. I told her no because I was not having a double mastectomy or hysterectomy at 34 years old. If I had the gene, that was not a guarantee that I would have cancer. My mom went forward with her prophylactic surgery. I fully supported her decision.

During that same time, I had a burning sensation in my right breast for months. It felt like someone was putting out a cigarette in my breast. I also started losing weight, which I loved because I was 13 pounds away from my goal weight. I looked ten years younger. Finally, one night, I grabbed my breast to soothe the pain. There was a lump. I made a doctor's appointment to be on the safe side. I did not tell my family because I did not want them to worry. I did not even tell my husband. My friends and family had their own priorities. I never wanted to be a burden or share concerning news. I did tell my boss because he was extremely supportive and more of a friend. I also wanted him to be aware of my upcoming medical appointments.

At the doctor's appointment, they performed a mammogram and said they did not see anything, but, they felt the lump. They decided to perform an ultrasound. During the ultrasound, the technician said that she was getting the doctor. At that moment, I knew something was wrong. I have had tons of ultrasounds, and they never bring in the radiologist. He said that he was concerned and I should see a breast surgeon. I scheduled my appointment with a surgeon. The breast surgeon did not think it was cancer because it was behind my nipple. She scheduled me for lumpectomy and encouraged me to take the BRCA gene test.

By this time, it was almost Christmas, and I just wanted to focus on making positive memories with family and friends, so I canceled the surgery. After all, the doctor did not think it was cancer. The lump was growing, but I was not letting it stress me out. I went to New York for my friend's birthday. We had a ball with the lump and all. When I returned from New York, the doctor asked me to come to her office to discuss the results of my BRCA testing. She shared the results that I was BRCA II positive. I told her the lump was getting bigger. She said that I needed to have the lumpectomy within two days. All I could think was who is going with me to the hospital because I had not told my family. I finally decided to tell Jeff and my mom. Well, if I told my mom, I told the whole family because she is a talker. Jeff and my mom were extremely supportive. My mom was disappointed that I was keeping all of that to myself. My surgery was on a Monday morning. My mom, Jeff, and my uncle were there. We prayed before the surgery. No complications during the surgery. The doctor said that the pathology results would be available that Friday. I was not worried one bit. No matter what the results were, I knew God had me.

On Friday, I hung out with my family and took the day off, waiting for the call to see if I had cancer or not. The doctor called me late Friday afternoon and told me that it was a very aggressive cancer and that she would tell me the details Monday morning. I know everyone handles things differently. I did not have a meltdown. I did not shed a tear. I called Jeff and told him because I was driving when I got the phone call. I do not know why I told him over the phone. As a matter of fact, I told everyone via a phone call or text message. I told my mom's oldest sister to call my mom for support because she was my mom's "counselor."

My mom's youngest sister was not receiving the news I kept telling her that it was cancer, and she kept telling me that it was not. That conversation sure made me laugh because she was adamant that her niece was not going to have cancer. My mom's middle sister reminded me that I was already healed. My mom's baby brother was there by her side, as always. As the news traveled, so did my friends. Some drove four hours to show their love and support. I refused to let cancer take my joy when I already knew that God had healed me. The party planner in me decided to have a Cancer Reveal Party, so the day after getting the news, I had a full blown party. We prayed, made vision boards, and laughed. It was a joyous occasion, not a pity party. I realized that people are going to react to news based on how your reaction. I could have said woe is me and have someone rub my back and say it is going to be ok OR I could trust the Lord and what His word says about healing and that is exactly what I did. The experiences of my cancer journey were nothing less than a miracle.

First, cancer treatment is an expensive process. Each chemotherapy session was twenty eight thousand dollars. The medicine to keep me healthy enough for the next treatment was sixteen thousand dollars. Thankfully, I was blessed to have treatment options. As a veteran I could obtain treatment through the VA hospital free of charge or through my employer. I chose to pay the five thousand and five hundred dollar deductible to have a renowned medical team save my life. My doctor suggested that I have a double mastectomy before beginning chemotherapy. My family encouraged me to get a second opinion. I am so glad I did. The second doctor suggested I begin chemotherapy first because she performed an ultrasound and determined that the cancer spread to my lymph nodes. She said that I had triple negative breast cancer and was stage II, so her priority was to save my life. I was on board with her decision. God gave me instant peace with the treatment plan. It only could get better from there, and it did. The plan was that I would have four months of chemotherapy, double mastectomy, total hysterectomy, and breast reconstruction surgery in less than a year. I was more excited about the free boob job. I was a saggy 36C. The doctor said I could pick whatever size I wanted, which was a 36DD. The boob upgrade was my priority throughout my entire treatment, LOL. Jeff and I would meet with the oncologist all my questions were surrounding my breast reconstruction like that was more important than being cancer free. I think it is important that when you are sick or even if you are a caregiver, you have to laugh, stay positive, and see the silver lining in everything. My silver lining was the boob job, and for someone else, it may be a trip to Jamaica after treatment. "A cheerful heart is good medicine, but a crushed spirit dries up the bones." (Proverbs 17:22 NIV)

In spite of my aggressive treatment, the outpour of love and support was astonishing. My job allowed me to work from home for an entire year. My co-workers donated over 300 hours of leave. One co-worker, in particular, was not a fan of donating leave and decided to give me a thousand dollars, which help cover the cost of my deductible. When my co-worker gave me the money, we were at my son's basketball game. The money was so unexpected and generous. All I could do was cry and thank the Lord for providing. My family, my friends, my co-workers, my husband's co-workers, my neighbors, and members from the church bought meals for our entire family throughout my treatments. Before my first treatment, I was getting a new ID card and the gentlemen making the card had numerous scriptures in his office. The Lord prompted me to tell him what I was going through. He said he had two things to tell me number one: I would have a powerful chemotherapy drug and that the treatment will save my life. Number two: I needed to reach out to an old friend and let them know what I was going through because they would help me during my journey. He did not know the name of the person, but he said it was someone I knew. Later that night, I reached out to 5 old friends and told them what was going on. One called me back and asked for my address. A week later, that same friend sent me five hundred dollars. She also committed to send money monthly. Glory be to God! I believe that man was a Prophet because just as he said that friend helped me, and I was on a strong treatment known as the "Red Devil."

Throughout my entire treatment, God was using people to remind me how much He loved me and how He was holding me in His arms. It did not stop there. I had a wait list for people wanting to go to chemo with me. One of my best friends shaved her head when I lost my hair. Speaking of losing hair, when you go through chemo you lose hair EVERYWHERE if you know what I mean, so it was nice not to have to shave for a while. My husband's co-worker cut her hair off and gave it to me. I was receiving cards, phone calls, and cancer gifts weekly. I call them cancer gifts because I had cancer at the time. People were blessing me with things constantly. I had gifts for my cancer treatment like wigs, hats, and blankets. I had gifts for after surgery like flowers, clothes, a peacock stationary, Pandora bracelet with charms, custom shirt, clothes, seat belt pillow to protect my upgrade, positive quotes, massage gift certificates, money, and journals.

My family and friends came to visit from Philadelphia, South Carolina, Colorado, New York, Maryland, and Florida. The amount of love I felt filled my heart to the point where it literally took my breath away. Imagine feeling so much love that your heart is so full that it is pressing against your lungs, and you cannot breathe. It sounds scary, but it is one of the most amazing feelings in the world. I was so full of love I felt like a sumo wrestler. I felt like I needed to walk with a wobble because I was full of pure joy. There would be times where I just wanted to be able to touch someone so the love would rub off on them and they could have just a little taste of what I was experiencing. God is a healer. God used what the enemy meant to destroy me to be the best experience of my entire life. Blessings on top of blessings on top of blessings. I was blessed from the top of my head to the soles of my feet.

One day, I just felt like being pampered and went to the nail shop. The owner asked how my treatment was going. I said fine. A customer who was a stranger offered to pay for my nails. I just cried tears of joy, and the owner decided to cover the rest of my bill. Now, this was nothing, but God. Not to sound racist, but my experience with Asian owned nail salons is that they never allotted me the opportunity to receive complimentary nail services or discounts of any kind. It was not because I had a nice smile or a regular customer. It was the favor of the Lord. Soon after that amazing experience, my mom's friend came to visit me. We had a nice visit. She gave me a wig and a card then told me to open the card after she left. I wanted to open the card immediately like on a brisk Christmas morning, but I did as she requested. The beautiful card contained five hundred dollars. I dropped to my knees, praising the Lord for him, keeping me physically, emotionally, and financially. Worrying does not do us any good. He cares for us. We need to trust Him and let Him love us.

Although, my cancer experience showed me what it was like to have unspeakable joy and peace that surpasses understanding. I had a few moments where I was sick and had indescribable bone pain, but I only cried two times. The first time was when my friend came from Florida to go to chemo with me, and my chemo got canceled because I had a fever. The cancellation impacted my entire treatment plan. It was more of a disappointment cry because it delayed my 36DDs. The second time was when I changed chemo drugs. My mom took me to the ER because the pain was intense. It felt like someone was carving in my bones in random places. The pain would move from my legs to my shoulders to my back. It was worse than childbirth. In those difficult times, God was with me. "The joy of the Lord is your strength." (Nehemiah 8:10 NIV) The goodness of the Lord and all the things He had already done gave me the strength just as His word says.

Despite the tears shed, Jeff earned "Husband of the Year." He worked his regular schedule and was my primary caregiver. After my double mastectomy, he milked my surgical drains. I am not going to go in detail to what that means because you may be eating right now, but it is not a fun job. He bathed and dressed me. Showers after major surgery are uncomfortable, but my strong husband washed me with a tender touch and compassion. He even dried my body with a hand-held blow dryer to make sure I was completely dry and comfortable. Jeff took care of all my needs and wants. In turn, our relationship went to a whole new level of love and intimacy. My breast and nipples were removed, but he still looked at me as if I was the most beautiful woman in the world. Jeff stayed true to his marriage vows. He loved me for better or worse and in sickness and in health.

Therefore, just as my Bishop prophesied to the congregation, God had so much more in store. God completely healed me from cancer. He did not just heal me but, He kept me. I would go to my doctor's appointments, and people would think I was a caregiver and not the patient. I was healed and whole. My hair grew back better than before. I did not look like I went through. I got my energy back and my spunk. I had a deeper understanding of God's power and grace. My perspective had changed. I had a new found appreciation for life and what really matters.

Life is not about chasing a dollar, keeping up with the Jones, and spending the majority of your day staring at a cell phone. We should spend time with our loved ones and live our God giving purpose. Life is short. The way God has orchestrated my life is incredible. He knew that I needed my marriage to help build my faith to have cancer-fighting faith. I can go a step further and say He knew I needed to know that He was love when I was a little girl to have faith enough to believe in whom God said He is. Thank you, Jesus! My cancer diagnosis was meant to uplift, encourage, and motivate others to continue to pursue their destiny. For those who do not know their purpose, pray, and ask God to reveal it to you. Lord knows, I am. I want to do His will. I want EVERY-

THING He has for me on Earth and in Heaven. Now, I will admit that I am sick and tired of these hot flashes and other minor health issues, but I am going to continue to trust the Lord in those areas as well. "For I am the Lord who heals you." (Exodus 15:26 NLT)

CHAPTER FOUR
GIVING

"A generous person will prosper; whoever refreshes others will be refreshed." (Proverbs 11:25 NIV) I have a little exercise. Please close your fist and take a moment to look at it. What do you see? Other than the fact that you may need a little lotion. I see limitations. A closed fist is not productive. It does not allow you to give or receive. You cannot even pick up a nickel on the ground with a closed fist. Now, open your hands and wiggle those fingers. What do you see now? I see possibilities. I see a supernatural increase and favor.

In truth, talking about money is a challenge for me because it makes me uncomfortable. I do not like asking people for money. I do not particularly appreciate when people ask me how much money I make, well maybe if I had a lot of money, it would not be an issue. In my opinion, money can be a sensitive topic, so this will be a short chapter. Nonetheless, giving is a biblical principle; worthy of an entire section. "Judge not, and you will not be judged; condemn not, and you will not be condemned; forgive and you will be forgiven; give and it will be given to you. Good measure, pressed down, shaken together, running over, will be put into your lap. For with the measure you use it will be measured back to you." (Luke 6:37-38)

You indeed reap what you sow. Please do not limit what you receive just to money. There are things in life better than money, such as peace, health, joy, favor, love, and rest. You can have millions in the bank and not have joy. What good is it to have tons of money, be miserable, and not bless others? Giving is an expression of love. God does not bless us just for us.

I remember an occasion, in which, I was picking up a few items from a local grocery store. The cashier asked the customer ahead of me to donate to the local children's hospital. The customer balled up his face and said, "No one has ever given me a dime, so I am not giving anything." The man picked up his groceries and began to walk out the door. The Lord put it on my heart to give the customer five dollars (The number five represents grace in the Bible). When I handed him the money, he looked on the ground first to see if the money fell out of his pocket, then he realized the money came from me. He relaxed his face and said "Thank you" with sincerity in his eyes. I do not know what happened to the man, but I pray that the small act of kindness changed him for the better. You never know how your giving can change someone's life.

We should give without the expectation of praise or a

selfish agenda. Building healthy partnerships is one thing, but your gift should not have a price tag. There have been times in my life that God has told me to give anonymously to friends and strangers. God knows our need even when the one giving does not.

His love for us never ceases to amaze me. Matthew 6:3-4 says, "But when you give to someone in need, don't let your left hand know what your right hand is doing. Give your gifts in private, and your Father, who sees everything, will reward you." His love towards us extends whether our hands are open to give or open to receive. I also believe that giving in private humbles you and allows God to get all the honor, praise, and worship. After all, He is the one that gave the seed to give in the first place.

"Bring all the tithes into the storehouse so there will be enough food in my Temple. If you do, says the Lord of Heaven's Armies, I will open the windows of heaven for you. I will pour out a blessing so great you won't have enough room to take it in! Try it! Put me to the test! Your crops will be abundant, for I will guard them from insects and disease. Your grapes will not fall from the vine before they are ripe, says the Lord of Heaven's Armies." (Malachi 3:10-11) It does not get any clearer than God's word that tithes (Ten percent of income) and offerings belong to Him. Tithes and offerings are the only areas in which God tells us that we can test Him. Jeff used to say, "You need to stop giving all our money to the church. We have bills to pay." I said, "Jeff paying our tithes and offerings is not an option."

Thankfully, he got on board and started to see the

windows from heaven opening up. For example, we could not afford to send our children to private school, but God allowed them to be awarded partial scholarships to attend the Christian private school of our dreams. "I will prevent pests from devouring your crops, and the vines in your fields will not drop their fruit before it is ripe." (Malachi 3:11 NIV) God was with me just before Christmas; I left my wallet in Toys R Us with three hundred dollars. I rushed back to the store, and the money was all there. I know that was nothing but the Lord and in direct correlation to our obedience in giving.

On another occasion, my debit card became compromised. God restored my account. I was shown favor when I went to Subway to pick up subs for dinner. I do not have to remind you that I rarely cook. When I got to Subway, the credit card system was down. I had the cash, but it was the only money I had until my new debit card came in the mail. The employee called the owner and told him about my situation. The owner said that the sandwiches were all free. All, I said was "Thank you, Jesus"! The owner did not know me. I was not a frequent customer. It was God again revealing himself to me. I later went back to the Subway with a thank you card, the money for the subs, and a tip. The owner was surprised. I believe showing my appreciation increased his generosity for future customers.

I know some may be thinking, "So what, you got a free five dollar foot long. What is the point?" The point is seeing the love in the gift no matter how big or small and being thankful.

CHAPTER FIVE
SERVING

"God is not unjust; he will not forget your work and the love you have shown him as you have helped his people and continue to help them." (Hebrews 6:10)

My son taught me a valuable lesson in serving. Jeff and I never volunteered to do anything in ministry. I remember church members asking me to serve and I would laugh and tell them I do not want to be serving in a ministry and a church member sees me cussing Jeff out on aisle 8 in the grocery store. Plus, I only knew one Bible verse. How could God possibly use me?

My son set a standard for our family and signed up to be a part of a ministry. When he signed up, I was so proud of him, but at the same time, I had to do some self-reflection. My mom has always told me that children are supposed to do better than the parents do, so I have always wanted to give them big shoes to fill. My little boy stepping up to the plate to be used by the Lord to serve encouraged me to follow. I think there is a verse in the Bible that says a child will lead them. My child did just that.

Once I signed up to volunteer at my church, I felt good about giving back to a ministry that has fed me spiritually, emotionally, financially, and physically. God was using me to be a part of something bigger than me despite ME. His love for us is beyond what we see in the natural. It is beyond what we think our limitations are. He has a purpose for us all. We need to step out on faith and pass by "our flaws" to serve. "For I can do everything through Christ, who gives me strength (Philippians 4:13 NLT)." Yes, we can. Serving comes in many forms.

For example, I have always had a passion for community outreach. I did not know how to get involved, but during a training program, I met someone who interned for a non-profit. The intern suggested that I volunteered as a mentor. I was nervous. I did not know the impact the mentee/mentor relationship would have on my life.

One thing that helped take the edge off was when the Mentoring Program Lead explained that I was not there to "save" someone. I was there to enrich a life. Those words have made a lasting impression and helped foster a life-long mentoring relationship with my mentee. It also reminded me that God is the one who saves. If He puts something on your heart, He will make every provision.

The Lord put it on my heart to conduct a coat drive. It started when I saw someone who needed a coat. I decided to donate to an entire family. I told my friends and family about the coat drive. The amount of support was astonishing. We had over 40 coats donated. We had extra coats to donate to a local shelter. "Feed the hungry and help those in trouble. Then your light will shine out from the darkness, and the darkness around you will be as bright as noon." (Isaiah 58:10)

With so much darkness in the world, serving others allows you to be a light. Light is captivating and contagious. The more I served, the more support I received. I started a Joy Closet at a local shelter. The purpose of the Joy Closet was to provide Christmas and birthday gifts to children in need, or allow the child to give a caregiver a present in celebration of a holiday or to say thank you. It is essential that kids understand the importance of showing appreciation to their loved ones at an early age. My sister even took time out of her busy schedule to assist with purchasing gifts to fill the Joy Closet, and several people provided funding, which enabled us to have a successful program.

Even though serving others is an opportunity to share and receive God's love, I want to be clear that our good deeds are not what gets us to heaven or even create heaven on Earth. We cannot work, pay, or be "good enough" to make it to heaven. We simply need to receive God's love and His finished work at the cross. "Let us labour therefore to enter into that rest, lest any man fall after the same example of unbelief." (Hebrews 4:11 KJV) We need to "work" on trusting and believing that God is love. God does not want us to worry and stress about anything. If you apply for a job and you do not get the job, do not worry. That means there is a better opportunity for you somewhere else. He always has our best interest at heart. "For even the Son of Man came not to be served but to serve others and to give his life as a ransom for many." (Mark 10:45 NLT) If you are tired of being tired, if you are feeling unloved, if you are depressed, if you doubt your purpose, if you want to receive Jesus Christ as your Lord and Savior, please say the following prayer:

"Lord, forgive me for my sins. I believe you died on the cross for my sins and rose from the dead on the third day. I receive your gift of salvation and accept you as my Lord and Savior. Thank you for bearing my sins and giving me the gift of eternal life. Come into my heart, In Jesus name, I pray. Amen."

"If you declare with your mouth, "Jesus is Lord," and believe in your heart that God raised him from the dead, you will be saved. For it is with your heart that you believe and are justified, and it is with your mouth that you profess your faith and are saved." (Romans 10:9-10, NIV) Glory be to God! Praise the Lord! You are saved! The angels are rejoicing in heaven.

If you said that prayer, please find a grace-filled word proclaiming church to grow your relationship with Jesus. Once you accept the Lord, please know that there will be challenges in life, but you are not alone in the process. In fact, you already have the victory. God gives us the victory through our Lord Jesus Christ.

Now, just let Him LOVE you.

AFTERWORD

The purpose of this book was not for me to air my dirty laundry or to satisfy all the senses of the flesh with more drama. We see enough of that on TV. Trust me, I had more drama filled stories to tell and elaborate on, but God was using me to lift Him up and touch someone's spiritual senses. This book is compact. Quality over page count. If one person's life was changed, these few pages were all that was needed.

I started writing this book as if I would be a best-selling author, not because of the fortune. I mean that would not hurt. I want people to know and believe that God is love and that He loves us to the uttermost depths of the universe or should I say to the last number (inside joke for my mom). There is no last number. Just as counting is unceasing, so is His love.

During the final moments of this book project, the enemy tried to plant seeds of doubt regarding this project. The

AFTERWORD

thoughts were negative such as, no one cares about God healing you from cancer or blessing you with free subs, but God had prepared me because through the course of this book I received confirmation after confirmation.

In the Faith chapter, I could not think of a verse to solidify my point. Then all of a sudden someone in the office who has never come to my desk started talking to me and mentioned the story of Jesus picking up mustard seeds on the side of the road in the Bible. What are the chances?

Also, in the Faith chapter, when I was discussing divorcing Jeff at the ten-year mark, I met someone the day I wrote that sentence who divorced after ten years of marriage. I wish I had finished the book prior to their divorce. As I wrote a sentence on faith, someone called me to tell me to encourage someone else due to my level of faith.

On several occasions, the scriptures used in the book were scriptures I heard in a sermon or read in a daily devotional the day after I wrote the scripture in my book. The day the book was to be completed, God led me to my editor. Out of all the days in the year, I was prompted to speak with her. God used her to bless me. The crazy thing is people kept asking me why March 14th was the day to finish the book (actually finished March 15th). I saw the number one day and said that is the date, but God knew that was the day I would speak with my editor.

One Sunday at church, we had a guest Pastor. Twice during her sermon, she said, "If God told you to write a book; finish the book." Jeff and the kids looked at me like wow she is talking to you. One of my sons asked if she knew me.

AFTERWORD

Those incidents were not a coincidence. The Lord was using people to speak to me and encourage me to do what He set in my heart to do. Do what the Lord is leading you to do even if you do not fully understand the bigger picture. There will be challenges reaching your purpose. Please persevere because your purpose may be the very thing to push someone to theirs.

ABOUT THE AUTHOR

 Tonya McDowell is a Christian with a passion for serving others. She is a United States Air Force veteran. Her commitment to service extends to her local community. She provides guidance and life skills to children through a local mentoring program. A two-time recipient of the President's Volunteer Service Award. Owner of Fowlkes Eagle Publishing, LLC aimed to provide publishing consulting services to authors ready to turn manuscripts into manifestations. Tonya is a proud Saint Leo University alumna with a Bachelor of Science degree in Computer Information Systems as well as a Master's of Business Administration (MBA).

Tonya is happily married (most of the time) to Jeff and lives in Virginia with her two teenage sons. She enjoys shopping, traveling, and more shopping. Her passion is to spread the good news of God's love for us all.

You can connect with me on:

📷 instagram.com/tonya.mcdowell.lethimloveyou

www.ingramcontent.com/pod-product-compliance
Lightning Source LLC
Chambersburg PA
CBHW071222070526
44584CB00019B/3118